A LATCH
AGAINST THE WIND

A Latch Against the Wind

POEMS & ILLUSTRATION
BY VICTORIA FORRESTER
ATHENEUM   1985   NEW YORK

Library of Congress Cataloging in
Publication Data

Forrester, Victoria.
  A latch against the wind.

  SUMMARY: A collection of poems expressing
the author's vision of the world.
  1. Children's poetry, American.
[1. American poetry] I. Title.
PS3556.07395L3   1985   811'.54   84-21526
ISBN 0-689-31091-9

Text and pictures copyright © 1985
by Victoria Forrester
All rights reserved
Published simultaneously in Canada by
McClelland & Stewart, Ltd.
Type in text and on jacket was handset
by the author in Centuar and Arrighi faces.
Printed and bound by Kingsport Press,
Kingsport, Tennessee
Designed by Victoria Forrester
First Edition

For the Thorntons
of Taucross Farm
        in token of a dream

And for my husband and son
        with my love

Like Mushrooms by the Door at Dawn

But poems are not *alive,* some say;
I beg to disagree.
Like mushrooms by the door at dawn
Their lives appear to me.

They spring unnoticed, out of sight;
Pray, view them tenderly;
The little mushrooms of the mind
Prefer obscurity.

Opening

A bolt of black—
Whole yards of it—
Yet tightly rolled,
The night.
How differently
A day is spread—
Like one great parachute
Of light.

The Day Began Like Dandelions

The day began like dandelions;
It floated breathlessly.
The cat observed in silence;
The birds made stitchery.
They worked a dandelion design
Of linen finely drawn,
A white on white embroidery —
The filigree of dawn.

Fairy Glen

The entrance to a fairy glen
With every stone to scale?
I never saw the evidence —
Just an established trail.

Dew

From elemental zone it slipped;
The dew, like spirit-stone,
Into a thousand pieces broke
And spoke in one clear tone.

Butterfly Cloth

How fragile
Floats the butterfly,
A banner barely cloth.
Woven of sterner stuff
It seems,
The tapestry of moth.

Cheshire Dawn

They pounced on me
And there they sat,
The purring sun
And the rising cat.
And it stayed with me
As the day wore on,
The indelible smile
Of Cheshire Dawn.

Midsummer's Eve

Midsummer's Eve is to the year
Surprising as a bird—
A delicate vibrato,
An understated word.
The door was closed in winter,
Still silent in the spring,
But crickets
Slipped the cuckoo's latch
So the Great Clock
Could sing.

Giddy Grace

An airy conversation,
It winnowed none the less.
Words flew in odd directions;
Some reached the wrong address.
A thousand words were spoken,
Yet hidden in them all
Was love, a seed unbroken;
Superlatively small,
It filled the air
With giddy grace
Like a high-bouncing ball.

Aviary

The leaves arrived
Like singing birds:
Behaving less like tree,
They made what late
Was merely branch
Into an aviary.

At Hinge of Day

I saw the sun
New-minted rise
At hinge of day.
We met
And bowed,
The Day and I;
Not eye to eye
Took we the measure
Of our match,
But sky to sky.

Cherry Wand

I can't say when the blossoms came
Or when they ceased to be.
They merely opened like a hand
That sets a young bird free.

With cherry wand the tree unfurled,
Released in every stem
Its brief instruction to the world,
Spring's fragile apothegm:

One can't outwit the wind, and yet
To be, merely To Be...
This cherry wand can hold back Time
And let pass — Ecstasy.

So Penetrant a Light

Love is to life
As after is to rain;
I've seen it pass through
Birth and death,
Make prism out of pain.
So penetrant a light,
So pure its substance
Seems to be,
All window shutters
Only prove
Their insufficiency.

How Take the Measure of Delight?

How take the measure
Of Delight?
By what authority
Do those who hold its value
Slight
Assay its quality?
Like feathers in an angel's wing
The smallest Joy may give,
Even to life's renunciate,
This one commandment—Live!

Don't Ask Me Who I Am

Don't ask me who I am;
I'll slip away,
Uncaught by convoluted monologue;
We'll meet another way.
Our souls are freer than all birds;
I'd rather be forgot
Than find myself tied into words
As solidly as knot.

Hours

Most hours drone
Like arbor bees,
Yet to a few belong
The mystery of melody,
The certainty of song.

A Room Full of Nobody

A room full of Nobody
Yet quite enough for me.
I'll listen to
The thoughts that call—
Sufficient company;
It's only in an empty shell
One dances with the Sea.

Runic Birds

Sandpiper steps
Imprint the sand:
Read backwards
In a line,
They seem to fly
Like runic birds
Beyond the shores
Of time.

A Bit of Night the Spider Seemed

She claimed the air
As spider ground,
Drew battle lines exact;
She drew the lines
In hex design,
As if the air were cracked.
A bit of night
The spider seemed,
Suspended in mid-day;
As frozen as a witch's frown,
As ominous, her sway.

!

Poems are akin
To the mere explanation
Of our days
As line to dot.
The quickening line forgot,
Existence spoken plain:
Where is the candlewick
Of life?
Where is the flame?

Autumn's Rein

I feel the pull
Of Autumn's rein:
In every leaf I see
The turning
Of the hemisphere
Toward Antiquity.

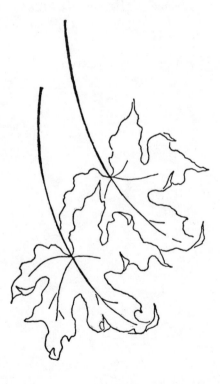

Migrant Birds

I watched the migrant
Birds return.
They settled on the tree,
As orderly as fence posts,
Recurrent as the sea.

Fog

The fog like a white stag appeared —
As sudden to the eye.
It formed itself as legends form —
Made antler out of sky.
Nor was it without chronicle;
Long sentences of sea,
In cadence like an ancient rhyme,
Ascribed it poetry.

Autumn Gold

Through autumn openings
The sky peered down;
Small, crooked spectacles
Were part of every tree —
On every hand the prospect
Of possibility.
I stooped to curiosity;
For autumn gold I panned
And held as lightly as a leaf
September in my hand.

Time Skein

The kettle hums;
My mother, singing,
Comes to me
Across the hours:
Time, like a magician,
Spinning,
Turning saucepans
Into stars.

I Hold October to my Eye

I hold October to my eye,
Frost faceting the grass;
The autumn days
Like beads appear;
The crows in circles pass.
The very air is amulet —
A talisman is passed.
I hold October to my eye
Like amethystine glass.

Pines

I walked with pines
Along the trail,
And all the way they gave
Assist of wing
Like angels' song
Or like a crested wave.
There lives a spirit
In the pines
Ancestral as the shore,
Both evergreen
And ever-grey
And almost evermore.

At Winter's Gate

At winter's gate
A lamp is hung;
Not distant like a star,
But wide as all
The world's great heart
October evenings are.
Horizons seem to fall away;
A spectral vision plays
Beyond the mind's imagining...
A flickering of days.

Treasure

At first, truth seemed
A treasured thing;
Now treasure seems to me
The magic which facilitates
Love's gracious poverty.
Like diamond soaked in sunlight,
Truth sparkles in the mind
But disappears into the heart
A dewdrop at a time.

Three Gifts

A light indwells the Daffodil
Like music in a bell.
I listen to the Trillium
As to a fairy tale.
Ambiguous as parable,
Continuous as prose,
The gnarled hands
Of the Apple Tree
Are handing me a Rose.

Compline

The day is very
Full of day.
The night is
Full of night,
Except for dawn
And eventide
When all is emptied
Into light.

I Hear the Music of All Days

Like silver tuning forks they stand
Against infinity;
Inscribed against the winter sky
This spare calligraphy
Of branch and leaf and poetry.
I hear the music of all days;
The leaves adagio fall
And light as softly on the ground
As an abandoned shawl.

Solstice

The winter night
Is beautiful,
Gregorian the snow;
It falls as softly
As the chant
Cantate Domino.

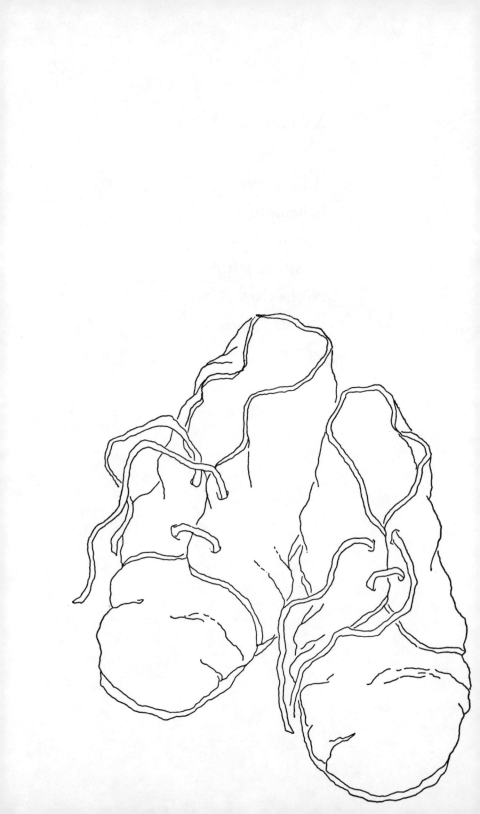

Sometimes Our Feet are Shepherd's Feet

The invitation was by star;
No scribe except the heart
Recorded what occurred that night,
Yet we can know in part:
Sometimes our feet are shepherd's feet
And life a manger rude;
Through half-abandoned doors
We glimpse
The brink of magnitude.

Nesting Boxes

The Months
Like nesting boxes
Lift
And leave behind
For Years to find
The precious sense
Of gift.

One Flower's Affirmation

One flower's affirmation:
A billion suns come up.
Molecular as morning,
They brim the buttercup.
In mimicry of mustard seed,
They silently impress
My heart with celebration,
The majesty of "*Yes.*"

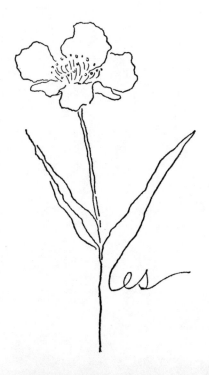

Sunset

Sunset is but
Bent rays of light,
Yet in bent light we see
The attitude of heaven
Before the Deity.

The Heart Admits the Firmament

The Heart admits the firmament,
Its habitat begun.
It weaves a latch against the Wind,
Makes portals for the Sun.
It dares not ask for company
Less common nor less vast
Than all the Stars in Paradise
Nor all the World at last.

Mending Stone

Where yesterday is
I will someday be . . .
Were ever words
More stone?
But it was stone
Love rolled away;
I'll use these
For its throne.